S0-ANF-353

50 Ways to cure a HANGOVER

50 Ways to cure a HANGOVER

Cara Frost-Sharratt

spruce

AN HACHETTE UK COMPANY

First published in Great Britain in 2011 by Spruce
a division of Octopus Publishing Group Ltd
Carmelite House, 50 Victoria Embankment, London, EC4Y 0DZ
www.octopusbooks.co.uk
www.octopusbooksusa.com

This edition published in 2017.

Distributed in the US by Hachette Book Group, 1290 Avenue of the
Americas, 4th and 5th Floors, New York, NY 10104

Distributed in Canada by Canadian Manda Group, 664 Annette Street,
Toronto, Ontario, Canada, M6S 2C8

Text and Design © Octopus Publishing Group Ltd 2011, 2012, 2017
Illustration © Jason Ford 2011, 2012, 2017

All rights reserved. No part of this work may be reproduced or utilized in
any form or by any means, electronic or mechanical, including
photocopying, recording or by any information storage and retrieval
system, without the prior written permission of the publisher.

ISBN 978-1-84601-547-2

A CIP catalogue record for this book is available from the British Library.

Printed and bound in China

10 9 8 7 6 5 4 3 2 1

NOTES

This book contains the opinions and ideas of the author. The author and
publisher disclaim all responsibility for any liability, loss or risk, personal
or otherwise, that is incurred as a consequence, directly or indirectly, of
the use and application of any of the contents of this book.

Contents

InTroduCTioN

If a normal Saturday morning involves waking up with the room spinning, while your head is pounding and the inside of your mouth tastes like a festering swamp, you've picked up the right book. Only the most cunning drinker can accurately figure out which tipple will tip them over the edge and know when to call it a night. For the vast majority, a big night out turns into a hangover the next day and that means endless hours of misery as your body tries to recover from the excess of the night before.

It seems unfair that a few drinks in the bar can leave you feeling like you've been run over by a steamroller, but that's life. Unless you become a teetotal hermit, chances are there'll be plenty of mornings spent leaning into the abyss of the toilet bowl or staring blankly at daytime TV. While you shake, retch, sweat, and gurgle, you'll probably

make rash promises about never drinking again.
But the miracle of short-term memory loss means
that as soon as the hangover mist has cleared, you'll
be making plans for your next big night out.

That's where this book comes in handy. There's
no point sitting around feeling sorry for yourself:
don't be harangued by your hangover—fight back.
We've gathered together 50 of the best
scientific, sensible, and downright silly
ways to beat the morning after. So,
now you can beat your hangover
before, during, and after you've
knocked back the beers. There
are tips on what to eat before
a mammoth drinking session,
how to pace yourself in the
bar, and midnight snacks that
will soak up the alcohol. And
since it's never too late for
victory over the hangover,
if you still wake up a little
worse for wear, you can
eat, drink, exercise,
and sleep your way
back to normality.

THE SCieNCe BiT

Everyone knows that if you drink too much alcohol, you'll suffer the next day. But what exactly does it do to your body, and why does it have so many nasty side effects?

Well, once you get down to the nitty-gritty, there's plenty of culprits hiding inside your glass of wine or beer, and the more familiar you get with the bottom of these glasses, the more likely you are to look and feel like death warmed over the next day. Ethanol is the main enemy of the drinker, and this is basically the alcoholic part of your drink. It might be cleverly disguised with hops, grapes, fruit, or syrup, but this is the little beast that's responsible for that pounding, spinning head. Ethanol dehydrates you, and if you don't top up with water while you're drinking, you'll feel the effects the next day. It goes without saying that the more alcohol you drink, the more dehydrated you'll get and the worse the hangover will be. Alcoholic drinks also contain congeners, which are toxic chemicals produced when alcohol ferments. These will add to your woes the morning after, but it's good to remember that, as a general rule, there are usually more of these in darker drinks.

Alcohol also tends to turn the straight-laced into the stupid, and it's easy to get carried away once your guard is down. A quiet drink after work can very quickly descend into a wild night of drunken abandon and debauchery. If there isn't a soft drink or a salty snack in sight, it should be no great surprise when you wake up in the morning with a pneumatic drill inside your head and a belly full of bowel trouble. When this happens, make sure that you have this book close to hand: when your blurred vision clears, you can flick through for some fast-acting remedies.

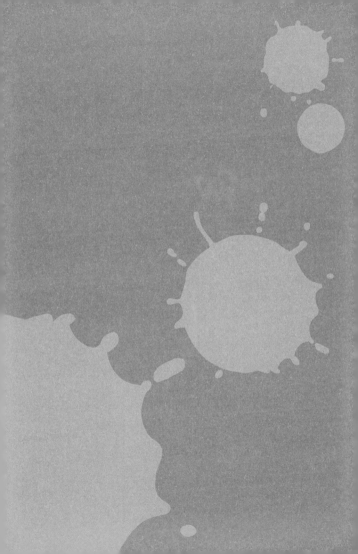

PrEvEntIon is BEttEr tHaN CuRe

1. Line Your Stomach

It makes sense to give your stomach something solid to work on before filling it with gallons of cheap, warm beer. An empty stomach absorbs alcohol into the bloodstream quicker than a full one and will definitely crank up the aftereffects of a big night on the sauce.

Forget any gourmet leanings: you need fuel food and carbs or fat to help put the brakes on a killer hangover. Try one of these for a slightly brighter morning after:

- **PASTA:** the protein and carbs combo in spaghetti Bolognese is perfect preparation.

- **CHICKEN:** the extra fat that comes with roast, barbecue, or schnitzel works wonders at lining the stomach.

- **BAKED POTATO:** any of your favorite toppings will do.

- **LARGE GLASS OF MILK:** a quick and easy solution for when time is limited.

2. FORWARD PLANNING

It's easy to think straight before you've poured a barrel full of beer and dubious-looking shots down your gullet. So, do the right thing and book a taxi home before you even leave the house.

When you go out in a group, appoint a designated driver to stay on the soft drinks. Failing that, plan your return journey in advance, so that your sober self can stay one step ahead of your drunken alter ego. Blurred and blighted by booze, you won't be in a fit state to call time on your drinking later on, let alone see straight to dial for a taxi. When the fine line between cheery drunk and debauched fool is approaching, the taxi driver (or designated driver) will come to your rescue and save you from memory loss and sidewalk snoozing.

3. LIMIT your SPENDING POWER

If you give yourself a cash budget and leave your cards at home, you can have a good night out that you'll remember the next morning. Short of ending the evening with a criminal record, there's no way you can get your hands on more money and drink yourself into oblivion.

It will take a bit of practice to perfect the cash allowance to hangover severity ratio. Also, there's a risk that this strategy could leave you with a reputation as a cheapskate. But it's a risk worth taking if you think about all the hangover-free days you can enjoy while your friends purge their stomachs and gaze at crippling credit-card bills.

4. Rein yourself in with pricey drinks

Ridiculously priced drinks are a guaranteed way to curb a hangover. Going to expensive bars means you'd need to remortgage your house to have a clear shot at drunkenness. When a cocktail costs more than your T-shirt, trips to the bar will be less frequent as the evening wears on. The obvious upside to being fleeced for a beer is a clear head the next morning so, if you choose your venue carefully, you could end the night as sober as you began it.

Of course, you'll still spend a king's ransom for your sprightly mood and glowing complexion, but you can always impress the opposite sex with your knowledge of trendy local bars —as long as they don't expect to be taken there.

5. Get a citrus pit Hit

In Puerto Rico, serious drinkers like to get a little bit fruity before they hit the booze. This quirky technique involves cutting a lemon in half and rubbing it all over the armpit of your drinking arm. This is worth a go for anyone who doesn't mind giving off the waft of a freshly sanitized toilet bowl every time they take a sip of their drink.

The Citrus Pit Hit should probably be tested in advance with the aftershave or perfume you're going to wear, as there could be a disastrous clash of aromas on the night. You might end up with your citrus arm pinned firmly to your side to avoid lemon-scented odor leakage. There is no advice on whether deodorant can still be worn, so anyone thinking about trying this technique should be vigilant about sweat rings and cleaning product body odor.

6. GO OUT WITH SENSIBLE FRIENDS

If you don't have any sensible friends, you'll have to take your chances with the hardened drinkers until they start settling down. But, as soon as any of your friends marry their under-the-thumb partners, get a serious job, turn into gym junkies, or have kids, make sure you put them on speed dial. These are the drinking buddies you need for liver damage limitation. With their low alcohol tolerance and need to escape from the bar before closing time, there's almost no chance of getting a hangover when you meet them for a drink.

The drawback is that you might have to talk about little Johnnie's potty training and sleep routine and witness the indignity of a grown man drinking nonalcoholic beer. But, whatever you do, don't be tempted to drown your sorrows: the only thing worse than a night out with a bunch of beer dodgers is the same night out followed by a hangover.

DAMAGE LIMITATION

7. HIT THE dance FLOOR FOR sobriety

This is only a good idea if you have a basic sense of rhythm, and it is definitely not advised for anyone with "dad-at-a-wedding" dance moves. But, if you can flail your limbs in vague time to a thumping bass line, then fling off your jacket and shimmy over to the dance floor.

This burst of energy will help you wear off some of the effects of the alcohol, but more importantly, it will keep you away from the bar area for a while. Ignore jibes from friends and remind yourself that if you're choosing to dance in the midst of a bunch of strangers, you could do with sobering up anyway. A word of warning, though: don't be tempted to show off your moves in a bar with no obvious inclinations as a disco—you'll just look like a first-class fool.

8. DON'T MIX AND MATCH

If the words "don't mix your drinks" have been ringing in your ears from the first time you went to a bar, you might wonder why you can't mix and match. What's the big deal about having a beer, followed by a shot, followed by a glass of wine? The truth is that that many people won't suffer any more the following morning just because they've had a glass of syrah in between their beers.

The problem is that, if you stuff your gut full of fizzy beer and then knock back a few creamy cocktails and half a bottle of red wine, your body is not going to thank you for it. The assault on your stomach lining is likely to end in you spending much of the night with the toilet as your new best friend.

9. Lighten up for Less of a Hangover

Have you ever noticed that you have a worse hangover if you've been drinking red wine? Well, there is some evidence to suggest that darker drinks do indeed lead to a worse head. While copious amounts of any alcohol will result in throbbing temples and spinning rooms, lighter-colored drinks should at least see that you make it out of bed the following day.

Red wine and dark spirits, such as rum, whiskey, and brandy, contain more chemicals than clear or light drinks. So, if you're planning to hit the bottle, try and keep your drinks as clear as you want your head to be the next morning.

10. spike your mood

If you think herbal remedies are for the vegetarian sandal brigade, then it's time to broaden your horizons and take a trip to the health food store. Ginseng is an ancient Asian remedy that's something of a wonder plant when it comes to perking yourself up after a drunken night out. This is one time when popping pills before going out to the bar is a good idea. Ginseng can help speed up the rate at which alcohol passes through your bloodstream, which should mean a quicker recovery time.

Alternatively, you can also take it the morning after, for a much-needed energy buzz. So, if you do have to get up and act like a valued member of society, keep some ginseng by your bedside, along with a glass of water, for a fast-acting pick-me-up.

11. soak it up with snacks

If personal grooming got in the way of lining your stomach before leaving home, all is not lost. There might still be time to minimize the effects of your boozy night out by munching some bar snacks in between sups of ale.

Olives, bread, and potato wedges are all fairly safe choices, but if you hang out in dodgy dives that are lacking in such gourmet snacks, just take what's on offer, down it all, and hope your body thanks you for it. Potato chips and nuts are packed full of salt, which will make you thirsty and likely to drink more. Having said that, a chip-fueled stomach is better than an empty one and no one's going to admire your designer shirt and new aftershave if you're covered in vomit.

12. Stretch your legs and sober up

You might think that the last thing you need after hitting the bottle on a Saturday night is a stroll home through your neighborhood streets at closing time. But, if you want to reduce your chances of needing to camp out in the bathroom in the early hours, a brisk walk can help take the edge off your drink-addled state.

Any delay between your last drink and passing out in bed will help limit your hangover. If you manage to resist flagging down a taxi you'll give your body a chance to start dealing with the alcohol and passing it through your system. Although you might not appreciate the late-night sightseeing tour at the time, you'll be slapping yourself on the back in the morning.

13. sneak in some soft drinks

It's not exactly rock 'n' roll, but alternating between alcoholic beverages and soft drinks is an age-old technique to keep a hangover at bay. Be as underhand as you want: offer to get an extra round, pretend you're drinking a spirit and mixer, or take a detour to the bar on the way to the bathroom.

Alcohol is a diuretic, which basically means that it gets rid of water in the body. Dehydration is one of the main symptoms of a hangover, so if you can nail this, you could be relatively clear-headed the next day while those around you are retching and crawling to the bathroom on their hands and knees. Fruit juice or water is the best option for an alcohol-interval drink, and this simple trick should leave you feeling pretty smug.

14. Refuel before you retire

Most people are delighted with themselves if they manage to end up in the right bed in the right house at the end of a major drinking session. Finding the bathroom instead of relieving your bladder in the closet during the night is an extra bonus. But if you can muster any functioning brain cells between shutting the front door and shutting your eyes, there is much to be gained from a quick detour to the kitchen.

Cups and glasses might be a step too far in terms of brainpower at this stage, but if you can find and turn on a faucet, you'll get a head start on your hangover recovery by gulping down some H_2O. Your dehydrated body will have something to work on while you sleep off the drinking session, and you might get some decent shut-eye. With a bit more effort, you could really put the brakes on the shakes and refuel your beer-logged stomach with a bowl of cereal or some toast.

Do iT

NaTuRa1LY

15. Pinpoint your Pressure

All you need for this hangover buster is an extra pair of hands. Depending on whether you disgraced yourself the night before, you might have a partner who is willing to help out.

Acupressure is an ancient Chinese healing art that pinpoints key pressure areas on the skin to help relieve pain and stress. A night on the sauce often leads to a fair amount of both, so it has to be worth a try. You're basically pressing buttons on your body to encourage it to heal itself, and if someone else is pressing the buttons, so much the better. It is possible to use acupressure on yourself, but the effort involved in finding a pressure point on a spinning head could prove too much for the seriously overindulgent.

16. SLEEP IT OFF

Sleep is one of the best ways to get over a hangover, but it's not always possible to spend the day under the blankets. Most people have commitments, but the effort involved in raising a hungover body from a warm bed can be gargantuan. A teetotal boss, an unsympathetic partner, or a demanding toddler isn't going to let you wallow in self-pity, which means you have to come up with cunning power-nap strategies.

You could offer to take care of the kids while your other half goes shopping. Once the front door closes, put on their favorite movie, shower them with candy, and doze off on the sofa while you "babysit." If work beckons, don a pair of dark glasses, pick a window seat on the bus or train, and catch some Zs on the way into the office.

17. Hit your hangover with herbs

You've probably never heard of feverfew unless you're an enthusiastic gardener with a nose for natural remedies. The name is a bit of a giveaway as to its healing properties, but even this might not tempt those who swear by heavy-duty painkillers. However, if you can prise yourself away from your usual headache-busting drugs, this pretty little herb might hold the key to hangover healing.

Feverfew is a natural painkiller that was traditionally used to treat headaches and fever. There's nothing in the rulebook about self-inflicted aches and pains, so if you feel like going *au naturel*, stock up on these tablets for those tricky mornings after.

18. Have ginger tea not black coffee

Vomiting is probably the worst hangover symptom.
There's nothing glamorous about spending the
early hours clinging to the toilet for dear life while
you become reacquainted with everything you ate
and drank during the evening. If you're lucky
enough to have an understanding partner, you
might get a pat on the head and the offer of a glass
of water once the contents of your stomach have
been flushed away and you've sworn on your
grandma's life that you'll never touch a drink
again. But before they open the cupboard, be sure
to ask for ginger tea. OK, so it does make you
sound like a carrot-munching, new-age bore, but
ginger is a classic remedy for nausea, and it might
stop your stomach from doing somersaults and let
you get back to sleep.

19. Build up a sweat

Ever wanted to lick your best friend's sweaty armpit? The answer is probably no, unless you have some deep-rooted and, frankly, disturbing fantasies. However, this strange post-drinking ritual was thought to be a sure-fire cure to the demon hangover by the Native Americans of yesteryear.

Instead of sleeping off a big night out, they would run around to build up a sweat, then would lick it off their bodies and spit it out—the idea being that the poisonous alcohol would come out in the sweat and their bodies would recover at a quicker rate. Maybe it did work, but more likely the thought of lapping up the morning-after excretions of your drinking pals was enough to banish the hangover anyway.

20. Feeling hot, hot, hot

A cleansing sauna is the hangover treatment of choice for drinkers in colder climates. Here's a cure that teeters on the edge of healthy living. In fact, take the alcohol out of the equation and you're almost treating your body like a temple. It's believed that the alcohol is sweated out by the intense heat, leaving your body free of toxins and ready to take another round in the bar.

Of course, hangovers and prolonged exposure to steamy heat don't always go hand in hand: no one wants to faint when a loosely wrapped towel is all that's keeping their privates private. If that, and the thought of being trapped in a sealed room with strangers seeping stale alcohol from their pores and excess flatulence from elsewhere, doesn't put you off, this could be a winner.

21. Blast away your Headache

Water should have a big part to play in any hangover remedy, and while you purge your insides with large glasses of cool water, you can also blast your wretched, aching body with it on the outside. Serial hangover sufferers know the benefits of a shower, and hardened drinkers will keep it icy cold for a short, sharp shock. If you're more of a wimp when it comes to water temperature, you can still reap the rewards of the power shower if you twist the control to "hot." The greasy face film, the bar smells, and the lingering traces of anything else unpleasant will disappear down the drain, and you'll emerge clean and refreshed.

If you really can't face peeling off your clothes and you're not going to come into close contact with other human beings for a while, you can achieve a temporary fix by splashing your face with cold water.

22. Work it off with a workout

You might think that only a crazed lunatic would jump out of bed with a hangover and go for a training session. However, if you're brave enough to give it a try, this is a good way to deal with the morning after. It could be the shock, the healthy blast of fresh air, the kick of endorphins, or just the self-satisfied gloat of the high achiever—it doesn't really matter why—it works!

By pulling on your sneakers and swapping your sheets for the streets, you are showing the world that you won't be beaten by a few glasses of Beaujolais and a late night. Pedestrians will cower as you run past leaving a trail of stagnant bar odor and the stench of your drenched shirt, which contains more pure alcohol than cotton. However, the morning workout means that you can slob, fart, belch, and eat crap food for the rest of the day with a clear conscience.

23. Arm yourself with artichoke extract

The vegetable might be an acquired taste, but you don't need to exercise your taste buds to take advantage of the healing powers of this fancy tonic. Although the idea of artichoke extract might sound a little left field, the thinking behind it isn't so crazy. The plant's leaves are believed to be able to help the liver digest alcohol and, as much as you want to fill your belly with beer when you're on a night out, you probably can't wait to get rid of it the next day. If you're still not convinced that vegetables can help with your hangover, combine this with water and food and you might be surprised at how quickly you start to feel human again.

24. Bury yourself in sand

A lot of people feel like burying their heads in the sand when they have got a pounding headache, a sandpaper tongue, and boiling bowels. But an ancient Irish hangover cure takes this to another dimension. When someone was suffering from an especially cruel hangover, they'd be buried up to their necks in river sand. It's not clear exactly how this helped with any of the symptoms—perhaps it just meant that their friends could escape to a safe distance so they couldn't hear the moaning and retching any more.

If you do want to try this out for yourself, remember that it's a lot of hard work to end up damp, cold, and immobile. And don't even think about it if you offended any of your friends in the bar the night before. Sand is heavy, and this is the perfect revenge for drunken insults.

25. Get jiggy with it

Alcohol can turn bashful blunderers into raging stallions when it comes to the bedroom. The bravado will be gone in the morning, and there will be throbbing in a very different area of the body, but that doesn't mean that a morning-after tumble under the sheets should be off the cards.

Indulging in a session of hangover sex might help ease the symptoms and kick-start your recovery. Even if your performance isn't up to the athletic antics of the night before, it will certainly take your mind off your hangover for . . . well, that depends on the severity of the hangover and the prowess of the sufferer.

26. sip a spoonful of milk thistle

It might sound like a quack remedy or something one of your "wacky" friends would tell you to take as a joke, but there's nothing funny about the therapeutic benefits of this prickly plant. Milk thistle seeds are part of an ancient medicine cabinet, and they are believed to help the liver deal with unwanted toxins. Whatever pleasure alcohol might bring while you're drinking it, it's an unwelcome guest as far as the body is concerned.

If you take a milk thistle tablet before you start drinking, it could help tone down your hangover by protecting your liver from the onslaught of poisonous alcohol that's about to come cascading toward it.

27. LET SOMEONE else DO THe Hard WORK

You will need all your powers of persuasion for this hangover buster, but if you have the gift of the gab and your partner is easygoing enough, this could be the cure for you. So, if you can still muster a winning smile among the bad breath and alcohol fumes, ask your long-suffering partner to give you a massage.

Headaches and aching muscles are part of the hangover package. The headache is a reaction to dehydration, while other muscle aches could be a result of overdoing it on the dance floor, giving your friend a piggyback, or any other antics that seem hilarious after a few beers but childish in the cold light of sobriety. A relaxing head and shoulder massage can work miracles on the physical side effects of an all-night binge.

28. Dip your spoon in the honey pot

A delicate stomach and a pounding head don't exactly do wonders for your appetite, and you're unlikely to feel like an elaborate breakfast when you peel open your eyelids the morning after. But even the most delicate constitution should be able to keep down a spoonful of honey. It's rich in potassium, which is exactly what your body craves after a night of heavy drinking, and there's no effort involved in eating it.

If you want to get creative, you could add it to your coffee or tea instead of sugar. Alternatively, spread it on toast for a double whammy of sweet-and-savory, sugar-and-salt action and feel your hangover hell dissolve.

29. stretch yourself

Hangovers can zap your mental, as well as physical, strength, so a good way to trick your brain into well-being is by occupying it with other tasks. While masochists do their penance running up mountains, you can take a more low-key approach to exorcising your drink demons by doing some gentle yoga or tai chi stretches. You don't even have to leave the house for this one: a DVD will save on public humiliation if you fail miserably or flatulence gets the better of you. You can also press the "pause" button if it all seems too much like hard work and you need to go back to bed for a rest.

CuLinArY CuReS

30. Sip ON BULL'S penis soup

How bad is your hangover? Is it bad enough to sip on a bowlful of bull's balls? There's no messing around in Bolivia: if you overdo it on the booze, *caldo de cardan* (bull's penis soup) is on the menu the next day. In fact, this popular broth is said to put a jolt in your sex drive and cure aches and pains as well, so it's a bit of a cure-all.

Although it's available in plenty of restaurants in Bolivia, bull's penis isn't an ingredient you're likely to see in the local grocery store in other parts of the world. So this particular hangover cure might have to be saved for a South American adventure. At least you'll know what to order when you go out looking for a hearty hangover cure.

31. Devour a hearty breakfast

A hearty breakfast has eased the torment of hangover sufferers for generations, and if you can face food, then this is the big daddy of the culinary "cures." Certain ingredients are vital for this strategy to do anything other than make you feel bloated on top of your existing ailments. Make sure you include the following:

- **BACON** for a protein punch.

- **TOAST** for carbohydrates and salt.

- **EGGS** for cysteine (this chemical can help break down the hangover nasties).

By combining all these belly-busting goodies on one plate, you'll give your hangover a good old kick in the gonads and send it slinking off in disgrace.

32. Rustle up some peanut butter on toast

The magic combination of protein from the peanut butter and the carb-loaded bread is at work here. Some food cures require a basic knowledge of cooking, but this simple snack is ideal for kitchen wimps and the plain lazy. No effort is involved in slapping huge dollops of peanut butter on a couple of slices of toast, and you could be on the road to recovery in a matter of minutes.

If this seems like a Herculean task when your insides are churning like a cement mixer, prepare a peanut butter sandwich before you go out in the evening, put it in the fridge, and it will be ready when you need it the next day. If opening a fridge is beyond your capabilities, then, unfortunately, you're a lost cause.

33. TrY SOmeThinG FiSHY

There can't be many people who would have liked to live in the Middle Ages. Apart from being mutilated for minor crimes and living ankle deep in mud and cow shit, you couldn't even enjoy a few after-work drinks without dreading the next day. There was nothing nice about hangover "cures" in those days, either: no ginger tea or freshly squeezed orange juice. If you were suffering the aftereffects of one too many tankards of Filcher's Pisswallop, you'd be presented with a platter of dried eel and bitter almonds.

Perhaps there is something to be said for this particular combination of protein and salt, but chomping through a mound of dry fishy chunks, that could send a diner's stomach into freefall when there probably wasn't much comfort in a bathroom in the Middle Ages, sounds like hell.

34. Revitalize on Vitamins

We all know that vitamin C can help fight off coughs and colds, but it can also help to fight hangover symptoms. If your brain cells went into meltdown and you didn't manage to hear your body screaming for fluids in the early hours, obey your thirst the next day and drink plenty of juice. Water is the ideal choice for rehydrating an alcohol-ravaged body, but vitamin C can actually help your liver deal with the alcoholic onslaught and remove the culprit from the scene of the crime.

Try mixing 7½ fl. oz. (225 ml) orange juice with about 3 fl. oz. (75 ml) cranberry juice for a really refreshing drink that hits the hangover spot, too.

35. Count on caffeine

A strong cup of coffee can help put a spring in your step when you're suffering from a hangover, and it's the remedy of choice for anyone who can't call in sick and has to drag themselves into work. Although coffee is dehydrating, it can have a short, sharp restorative effect on a fuzzy head and should at least make you look alert, even if you're feeling especially rough.

If you want an extreme caffeine hit, order a "Red Eye." It's a regular coffee with an added shot of espresso, and it will blast your hangover to hell and back. A "Black Eye" increases the shots to two, while those with serious morning-after issues can go straight for a "Dead Eye"—three shots of espresso. Warning: this is not for the fainthearted!

36. Do some armchair sports

If you can keep down liquids when you wake up in the morning, then you can work your way through a hangover without feeling like death warmed over. While strange noises and noxious substances will no doubt pour from your body all day, you can rehydrate and refuel with sports drinks.

Always choose a decent brand and not one that's aimed at sugar-addicted teens with too much allowance money to spend. Also, try to avoid fizzy drinks, as these will only help increase your gas output. Real sports drinks should contain everything you need to deal with dehydration, and as this is one of the main causes of a hangover, it's wise to get your fridge stocked in time for any big nights out.

37. Sip on cabbage cooking water

When Roman emperors got a little carried away with the booze, they'd deal with the sore head by gulping down a bowl of boiled cabbage water. So, if you overdid it at the toga party, you can follow in their footsteps and sip on the dregs of overcooked vegetables. If this doesn't have you making a beeline for the bathroom, you have got the constitution of an ox.

Of course, you'll smell like a nursing home if you opt for this "cure"; but who cares if it helps with your hangover. Let's face it, you look and feel like crap anyway, so what difference is a little *eau de cabbage* going to make?

38. Take a sweetener

We've heard about the restorative effects of honey, but how about drinking a cocktail of the sugary nectar with a generous dose of cider vinegar? This gut-wrenching combo might not sound too appealing, but anything's worth a try when the carpet between your bedroom and the bathroom is wearing thin from overuse.

These two ingredients are used in a variety of health tonics, and hangover sufferers in Iceland favor this particular remedy for a bad head and queasy stomach. Just mix a spoonful of each into a mug of warm water and sip slowly. At the very least, you're getting fluids back into your body.

39. Get fruity

When it comes to food, fruit is probably way down on your list of options for dealing with excessive alcohol issues. Although you're craving a plate of hot, fatty food, try reaching for the fruit bowl before you line your stomach with grease.

Alcohol zaps the body's natural store of potassium, and the humble banana is packed full of this essential mineral. It might not be the easiest thing to eat when you need a pair of pliers to peel your parched tongue from the roof of your mouth, but it's worth the effort. Have a glass of water to irrigate your desertlike mouth, then progress to a banana. Now you can move onto the fat feast.

40. KiLL
OR CURE

It's interesting that raw eggs seem to be eaten
either by die-hard body builders or die-hard
drinkers. Chances are you fall into the second
category if you're reading this book, but the raw
egg "cure" still has a certain kudos about it. The
big hit of protein from the intact egg yolk sliding
down your gullet should have an immediate effect:
it will either make you feel better or make
you throw up. It's not exactly a cheery
choice to make the morning after, but
you feel like crap anyway, so
what's the big deal?

PRAIRIE OYSTER
- 1 egg yolk
- Dash of Worcestershire sauce
- Dash of white wine vinegar
- Salt and pepper

Carefully place the egg yolk
in a small glass. Add the other ingredients and
season with a little salt and pepper. Down it in one.

41. Tuck into a Takeout

Anything hot, greasy, and cooked by someone else is bound to help with your hangover, and this is the dinner of choice for countless sufferers. If you missed out on the hearty breakfast because you were asleep or the thought of food was still making you sprint for the bathroom, the evening takeout will be the highlight of your day.

Pick your place on the sofa, line up some trashy TV, and order your usual meal from your trusted takeout of choice. This is no time to experiment with flashy menus that have landed on the doormat recently—save takeout trials for another night. Hangovers call for comfort food; good, honest plates of greasy goodness that will help soak up the remaining alcohol.

DIAL
PIZZA

42. Bag a bowl of chicken noodle soup

Do you remember your mom making you chicken noodle soup when you were sick as a child? Well, the restorative powers of this simple meal go way beyond toddler stomach bugs. Plenty of grown-ups with a love for the booze swear by this tasty bowl of goodness to get them through the worst of their hangover woes.

The classic combination of protein from the chicken, carbohydrate from the noodles, and some added salt works wonders for a food-deprived body. There are plenty of other "cures" that use these basic ingredients to combat the effects of alcohol, but none is quite as comforting as a big bowl of chicken noodle soup. Obviously, it needs to be served with lots of sympathy and cuddles to really have an effect.

43. Eat a canary

It's not an ingredient that you're likely to have lying around in your kitchen, but ancient Roman cupboards would have been crammed full of canaries. These crunchy little morsels were considered a delicacy at the best of times; they were thought to be especially helpful for hangovers. There doesn't seem to be any scientific backing to the benefits of eating small birds to cure a fuzzy head, but then logic doesn't exactly go hand-in-hand with drunkenness.

If you are tempted to tuck into your gran's pet instead of a takeout, you will need to prepare and cook it thoroughly and make sure there's a cat close by that can take the blame for your unusual hangover cravings.

Back on the Wagon

44. JOIN THE PROS

Are you a man or a mouse? Are you going to sit there shaking in the corner sipping on a mineral water, or are you going to stride up to the bar and order every movie star's favourite hangover cure? The Bloody Mary is the socially acceptable way to get drunk at breakfast, as the fruit juice and vegetable garnishes disguise the boozy beverage as a health drink.

BLOODY MARY

- 1 fl. oz. (25 ml) vodka
- 5 fl. oz. (150 ml) tomato juice
- Pinch of celery salt
- 2 drops Tabasco Sauce
- 4 drops Worcestershire sauce
- Squeeze of fresh lemon juice
- Pinch of ground black pepper
- Celery stick, to garnish

Put all the ingredients into a tall glass with some ice, mix well, and then add the celery stick to serve.

45. start WHERE you Left off

This is the hangover cure that separates the men from the boys. Amateurs shouldn't be tempted to try this out, especially in public. Drunkenness can return at the speed of light and, while crude jokes and vocal appreciation of the opposite sex are tolerated in crowded bars after midnight, managers aren't quite as laid-back in family-friendly restaurants at lunchtime.

If you can handle your beer, and you want a tried-and-tested way to get rid of your hangover, then order whatever you were drinking the night before. No low-alcohol versions to soften the blow; this is the hardcore hangover solution. Your taste buds and stomach might put up a bit of a fight for the first few sips, but just drink through it and worry about the hangover later on.

46. Jump in at the deep end

If you like champagne but can't resist the urge for a manly serving of stout, this hangover helper offers the best of both worlds. Creamy smooth Guinness is given a bit of a makeover with the addition of champagne, and the odd combination is a taste sensation. On this occasion, opposites really do attract, and you'll be back to your old self in no time.

To create your own Black Velvet drink, half-fill a champagne glass (or highball glass) with Guinness. Top up the glass with champagne, pouring it over the back of a spoon so it separates in the glass. And if you're too cheap to splash out on champagne, sparkling wine will do.

47. Have a short, sharp shot

A shot of alcohol is a great way to get the party started all over again. It's quick and easy to drink and will put a spring in your step before your body realizes that you're inflicting further punishment on it. If you're still feeling a bit queasy, it's best to steer clear of shots with lots of cream or flavored liqueurs in them; stick to something simple that will get the job done swiftly and painlessly, like a Lemon Drop.

LEMON DROP

- Sugar, for dusting
- 1 sugar cube
- 1 fl. oz. (25 ml) vodka
- 1 teaspooon lemon juice

Dust the rim of the shot glass with sugar, then drop the sugar cube into the bottom of the glass. Mix the vodka and lemon juice together with ice in a cocktail shaker and then carefully strain into the shot glass.

48. Order an Irish coffee

Who says you shouldn't drink alcohol or caffeine when you have a hangover? Well, some people do, but just ignore them if you want to give your taste buds a livener and blast away the morning-after blues. This hot drink has plenty of attitude and a large dose of warming spirit. Perfect for winter wipe-outs.

IRISH COFFEE
- ¾ fl. oz. (25 ml) whiskey
- 1 teaspoon sugar
- Mug of freshly brewed coffee
- Thick cream, to top up

Add the whiskey and sugar to the mug of coffee and stir well until the sugar has dissolved. Carefully pour the cream over the back of a spoon on top of the coffee so that it floats in a separate layer.

49. Fill your glass with bubbles

Champagne might be fancy, overpriced wine for some, but there's a lot to be said for sipping expensive drinks when you're recovering from the aftereffects of cheap ones. The bubbles will go straight to your head and help pep up your mood and, if you add a dash of orange juice, you can double your feel-good factor with a health-giving vitamin C hit.

If you have got a party that you can't worm your way out of the day after a regrettable night, the champagne solution makes perfect sense. The hangover will be put aside for another few hours and you might even enjoy yourself. Try to find a tactical position close to the canapé trays and you can line your stomach at the same time.

50. If all else fails . . .

Pull the blankets over your head, take the phone off the hook, draw the curtains, and write off the whole day in bed. Time is the only proven cure for a hangover that will work in every case, and sometimes there's no point in trying to get up and engage in normal life.

Before you begin your self-imposed isolation, you'll need to gather a few essentials: a bowl or an old towel in case last night's excess comes back for a second visit; a large bottle of water for rehydration; and a few snacks to keep hunger at bay. Once you're in your pit, Armageddon itself shouldn't rouse you.

Acknowledgments

Executive Editor: Sarah Ford
Senior Editor: Leanne Bryan
Copyeditor: Camilla Davis
Proofreader: Abi Waters
Americanizer: Caitlin Doyle
Design Manager: Eoghan O'Brien
Designer: Clare Barber
Illustrator: Jason Ford
Production Manager: Caroline Alberti